HALO, HALO, HALO!

AN ALTERNATIVE LOOK AT
THE CHRISTMAS STORY

BY MARTIN BAXENDALE

ISBN 0-9522032-0-0

Printed in Britain by Stoate & Bishop (Printers) Ltd,
Cheltenham & Gloucester: Typesetting by Alpha Studio,
The Old Convent, Beeches Green, Stroud, Glos.